Contents

SUMMER VIBES

GET READY FOR SUMMER

GET READY FOR
SUMMER

The Zoella Generation: GET READY FOR SUMMER

Essential DIY summer projects to make, bake & create. Fun, fashion & food ideas from lemon cupcakes to flip-flop foot scrub, customised sunglasses & tie-dye t-shirts.

Created By Christina Rose
Creative Direction: Daisy Bell

Image contributors: under license from Shutterstock

First published in the United Kingdom in 2016 by
Bell & Mackenzie Publishing Limited

ISBN: 978-1-910771-98-3

www.bellmackenzie.com

BELL & MACKENZIE
PUBLISHING LIMITED

SUMMER SNACKS & NIBBLES

♡

perfect iced fruit smoothie

you'll need...

200g chopped, peeled peaches (tinned peaches are fine)
200g chopped, peeled mango
1 tbsp lemon juice
2 tbsp honey
250ml water
Handful of ice cubes

now make it....

Place the peaches, mango, lemon juice and honey in a blender and whizz until it's smooth.

Add the ice cubes and blend for a few seconds longer.

Serve in a tall glass with a stripy straw and lots of sunshine.

peach
+
mango
+
lemon
+
honey
+
water

ENJOY!

BLEND

Layered Kiwi & Strawberry cooler

now make it....

Make the first layer by blending together the ingredients until smooth.
Pour this layer into a tall glass.

Give the blender cup a really quick rinse and then blend together all the ingredients for layer 2 until smooth.

Pour this on top of the first kiwi layer and drink right away.
It looks really cool and tastes really great!

you'll need...

For layer 1 you'll need :
1 peeled kiwi
1 medium banana
2 tbsp Greek vanilla yogurt
120ml milk

For layer 2 you'll need :
75g frozen strawberries,
1 medium banana
120ml milk

I ♡ SUMMER

NO-Bake summer cheesecake

This makes a single mini cheesecake. If you want to make enough for the whole family or friends just increase the quantities.

you'll need...

2 digestive biscuits
4 tbsp vanilla Greek yogurt
Handful of strawberries
1 tsp icing sugar
1 dessert cup or a small single serving bowl

now make it....

First crush the biscuits with a rolling pin. You can do this by putting them in a freezer bag and bashing (it means you won't get crumbs everywhere too).

Tip the bashed biscuits into the dessert cup and spoon the yogurt on top.

Chop the strawberries and sit these on the yogurt. Sprinkle with icing sugar and place in the freezer for about an hour.

After an hour it will be firm but won't be rock hard, so grab a spoon and dig in.

cheesy Picnic Garlic Bread

This is a great recipe to make and take outside for friends to share for a garden picnic or park party.

you'll need...

500g strong white bread flour
7g sachet/1 tsp fast-action yeast
1 tsp salt
300ml warm water
2 tbsp olive oil
1 tbsp clear honey
2 garlic cloves, crushed
25g soft butter
100g mature cheddar, grated
small baking tray (about 22cmx17cm)

now make it....

Place the flour, yeast and salt into a large bowl.

In a separate jug mix together the water, oil & honey. Then pour this honey water into the flour bowl, stirring all the time until you make a ball of soft dough.

Sprinkle some flour onto the worktop and knead the dough for 5 minutes until it no longer feels sticky (add a little more flour as you need it).

Now stretch the dough a bit so that it sits in the base of the baking tray.

Next mix the garlic with the butter, dot it over the dough and sprinkle over the cheese.

Cover the dough in baking tray with some cling-film and leave to rise for about half an hour. While the dough is rising heat the oven to 200c/fan180c/gas 6 (ask an adult to help you with the baking/oven part of this recipe).

Peel the cling-film off and bake the bread for 25-30 minutes until it's golden.

Cut into pieces and eat while it's still nice and warm. You can't beat fresh baked bread. Delicious!!

pineapple

GET READY FOR SUMMER

cheese & Pineapple Pop Tarts

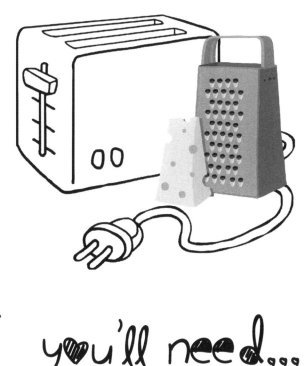

you'll need...

1 mini pitta bread
1 tbsp soft cheese
1 tbsp grated cheddar cheese
2 tsp chopped pineapple chunks

now make it....

First mix together the soft cheese, grated cheese and pineapple to make a spoon-able mixture.

Next toast the pitta bread in the toaster for 1 minute. (Get an adult to help you use the toaster if you need to).
Pop the pitta out and slice a small opening at one end. Use a spoon to push your cheese & pineapple mixture through the opening and then gently squash the pitta closed between your hands.

Put it back in the toaster with the opening pointing up so the filling doesn't fall out. Toast for 1-2 minutes until golden and crisp. Enjoy but be careful when you bite into it as the filling can be really hot.

Delicious!

This is a perfect 'grab & go' sunshine snack.

HOMEMADE Lemonade

Homemade lemonade is a truly authentic American style drink. To make it look supercool serve it in a mason jar with a straw and some fresh mint.

you'll need...

½ lemon (or 2 tablespoons of lemon juice)
1 tablespoon sugar
250ml water
Handful of ice cubes
Blender

now make it....

Rinse the lemon well, remove any pips and chop. Add everything to the blender, twist on the blade and blend until smooth.

Tip: Alter the amount of sugar to get the taste right. You could add some strawberries too for pink lemonade.

Lemon cupcakes

Nothing says summer quite like lemon does. Pair these delicious cupcakes up with some homemade lemonade too! See recipe on p12

now make it....

Heat oven to 180C/160C fan/gas 4.

Leave the butter out at room temperature to make sure it's soft and place 12 fairy cake cases into a cake tin.

Beat the butter and sugar in a bowl until it's really soft, then add the lemon zest. Slowly stir in the eggs, then fold in the flour until it's all nicely combined and smooth.

Divide the mixture into the cake cases. Bake for 18-20 minutes or until the cakes are golden. Remove them from the oven and leave to cool on a wire rack. (Ask an adult to help you with the baking/oven part of this recipe).

While the cakes are cooling make the buttercream icing. To do this just beat the butter until it is really soft and gradually add in the icing sugar, juice & lemon zest.

When the cakes are completely cool spread the buttercream on top and decorate with your sprinkles.

you'll need...

For the cupcakes you'll need .
140g unsalted butter
100g caster sugar
zest of 1 lemon
2 large eggs
140g self-raising flour

For the buttercream you'll need .
85g butter
175g icing sugar
zest and juice of lemon
Lots of sprinkles or sweets, to decorate

strawberry sunshine sandwich

strawberries in a sandwich sounds CRAZY but it's actually lovely. Give it a try.

♡ you'll need...

2 pieces of bread
1 tablespoon cream cheese
3 or 4 strawberries
sprinkle of caster sugar

now make it....

spread the cream cheese over the bread like butter.

slice the strawberries and arrange them on top of the cream cheese on one of the slices of bread. sprinkle the sugar over the strawberries and close the sandwich with the other piece of bread

cut into 4 and eat straightaway before the strawberries make the bread soggy.

very strange but totally scrumptious.

sweet cheerio snack Bars

now make it....

Line a small baking tray with baking parchment.

Place the butter and marshmallows in a bowl and cook in the microwave for about 2 minutes or until the mixture is melted. Make sure it doesn't burn.
(Ask an adult to help you with this part of this recipe).

Add the cheerios to the melted marshmallows and stir well until every hoop is covered with the sticky butter and marshmallow mix.

Pour into the baking tray and gently press down with the back of a spoon until it's even and level.

Leave to cool, cut into bars and share with your friends & family.

you'll need...

3 tablespoons soft butter
200g mini marshmallows
100g cheerios

GET READY FOR SUMMER

watermelon stars

you'll need...

Half a watermelon
Handful of blueberries
sprinkle of icing sugar
star shaped cookie cutter

now make it....

Place your watermelon half flat side down and cut it into thick slices about 2cm wide.

Lay the slices down flat and cut out star shapes using the cookie cutter (only use the red flesh not the green rind).

Place the watermelon stars in a bowl along with the blueberries. sprinkle with icing sugar and serve straightaway.

super simple Lemonade Ice Lollies

> Okay, this is by FAR the easiest recipe you will ever make.

you'll need...

Ice lolly moluds
lemonade (or a juice of your choice)

now make it....

Pour your lemonade into your moulds, pop on the lid and they are ready for the freezer. Leave them in the freezer for at least 5-6 hours but preferably overnight.

super easy and super tasty!

watermelon sharing punch Bowl

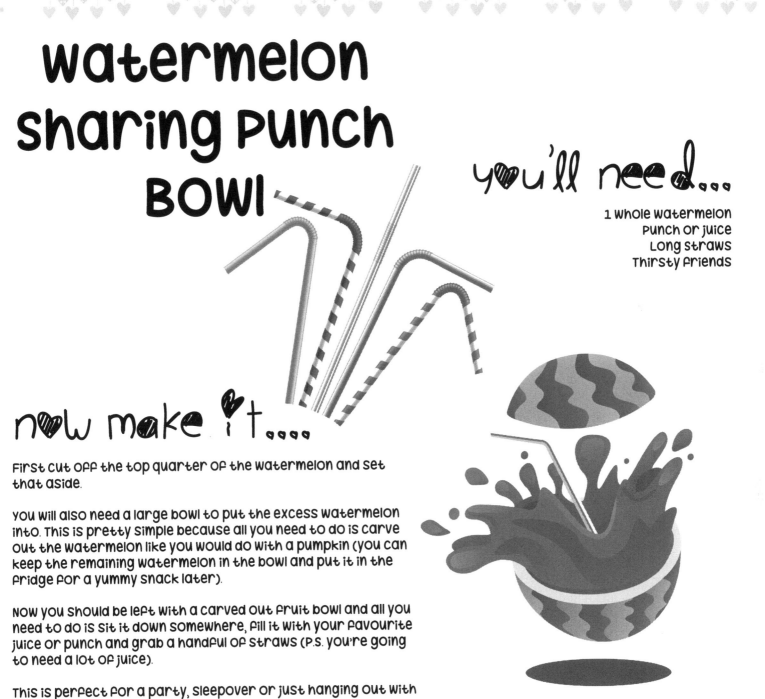

you'll need...

1 whole watermelon
punch or juice
Long straws
Thirsty friends

now make it....

First cut off the top quarter of the watermelon and set that aside.

You will also need a large bowl to put the excess watermelon into. This is pretty simple because all you need to do is carve out the watermelon like you would do with a pumpkin (you can keep the remaining watermelon in the bowl and put it in the fridge for a yummy snack later).

Now you should be left with a carved out fruit bowl and all you need to do is sit it down somewhere, fill it with your favourite juice or punch and grab a handful of straws (P.S. you're going to need a lot of juice).

This is perfect for a party, sleepover or just hanging out with your friends.

FRO-YO LOLLIES

you'll need...

Petit Filous yoghurts
Lollipop sticks
A sharp knife

now make it....

Take the knife and carefully make a really small slit (just a couple of millimeters) in the centre of the film at the top of the yoghurt pot.

Slip one of the lollipop sticks slowly though the hole until it touches the bottom of the pot and is sticking straight up.

Place the pot and stick in the freezer and leave to freeze overnight. When it's ready, peel the lid and hold onto the stick as you squeeze the base of the pot to get your fro-yo out in one piece.

Delicious ready-made fro-yo lollies don't get any easier than this!!

This is insanely easy to do and the results are great.

summer smoothie Dessert

you'll need...

100g frozen blueberries
100g frozen raspberries
1 tablespoon greek yogurt
1-2 tablespoons honey
3 tablespoons chopped fresh fruit
1 tablespoon granola

now make it....

Put the raspberries, blueberries, honey and Greek yogurt into a blender and whizz it all up together. You may need a little liquid to loosen everything up so feel free to add a splash of water or almond milk.

Tip your blended smoothie into a bowl and top with chopped fresh fruit and granola sprinkled all over.

HANDCRAFTED COOKIES

GET READY FOR SUMMER

summer sprinkle cookies

now make it....

Heat oven to 200C/180C fan/gas 6.

Leave the butter out at room temperature to make sure it's nice and soft.

In a bowl mix the butter, caster sugar, egg yolk and vanilla extract together until it's creamy. Then mix in the flour to make a ball of cookie dough.

Divide the dough into about 10 small balls rolling them in your hands. Place on a baking sheet and bake for 12-14 minutes or until golden, then leave to cool. (Ask an adult to help you with the baking/oven part of this recipe).

While the cookies are cooling, mix the icing sugar with a few drops of water to make a thick but runny consistency.

Dip each biscuit half into the icing, then straight into the sprinkles and leave to dry on a wire rack for a long as you can bear it before digging in.

you'll need...

90g butter
25g caster sugar
25g icing sugar
1 egg yolk
1 tsp vanilla extract
150g plain flour
70g icing sugar, sifted
lots of sprinkles

GET READY FOR SUMMER

FUN IN THE SUN

GREAT THINGS TO MAKE & DO

summer memory jar

you'll need...

clean glass jar with lid
1 piece of ribbon or twine
newspaper or printed letters
glitter
PVA glue/mod podge
paint brush
post-it notes

now make it....

Print out or cut out enough newspaper letters to spell the words "MY SUMMER" and put them to one side.

Use the brush to apply a thin layer of glue around the outside of the jar. Now press the letters onto the glue around the jar to make the words "MY SUMMER".
Then tie the ribbon or twine around the neck of the jar to make a bow. Nip off any ends that are too long.

Now add anything you like to remember your summer by. Try post-it notes filled with your everyday thoughts and events along with keepsakes, ticket stubs or souvenirs.

When the summer is over, seal it up and don't look at it again for a whole year. When you do you'll be amazed at the memories that come flooding back when you read or look at one of the mementos you've saved.

Clothes Line Photo Frame

now make it....

First take out the glass and back of the photo frame, you won't need either of these, it's just the wooden frame itself you'll be using.

Then, depending on the size of frame you are using, decide how many strings you want to hang photos from within the frame. It might be 1,2 or 3. It really depends how big your pictures are.

Turn the frame over so you are looking at the reverse side. Evenly space the eyelets down the left hand side of the frame and tap them in with a hammer. Measure the distance between each eyelet and repeat on the right hand side of the frame so that your string will hang straight.

Feed the string between the eyelets, tying the knots tightly to hold in place.

You should now have an empty photo frame with string 'washing lines' stretched across it.

Hang the frame up on the wall. Grab your favourite polaroids or pictures and hang these on the strings using wooden clothes pegs. It's a lovely DIY to keep your summer fun pictures in.

you'll need...

HAND MADE WITH

Large wooden photo frame
string
Frame hanging eyelets
wooden clothes pegs
Ruler
Pencil
Hammer

POOL Party Photo Booth

This is how you can make your own summer pool-party themed photo booth.

you'll need...

A large piece of neon fabric
Drawing pins
Some friends or family (obviously),
some really cool/cute pool inflatables (you can get lots of awesome/cheap pool inflatables on amazon!)

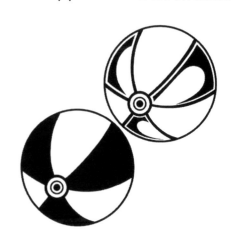

now make it....

Just pin up your large piece of fabric on a wall of your choice using drawing pins then angle your camera/phone so it looks like the whole frame is bright neon fabric. Get into your costume, grab your inflatables and use your imagination to get creative and come up with some epic photo shoot poses you can post everywhere!

Holiday Beach Jar

Everyone collects shells and pebbles at the beach and usually they just end up getting lost in a drawer with old make-up and paperclips. This is a way to keep those precious finds special.

you'll need...

1 jar with a lid
Time on the beach to collect your stuff
Sticky label

now make it....

Put some sand in the bottom of the jar and add whichever cool pebbles, shells or memorabilia you can find. (If you are on holiday try adding a small postcard or travel tickets too, to turn it into a mini time capsule of memories).

Once you have put your stuff in it, label the jar up with the place and date & put it onto your shelf. Over time you can make a collection of beach jars and line them up to make a cool display.

GET READY FOR SUMMER

Holiday Map Art

This makes a really cool art piece for your room that will get lots of comments.

you'll need...

Map
Photo frame
Embroidery needle
Brightly coloured embroidery thread

now make it....

Get a map of your holiday destination or just a special summer place. Either use a map of the your own country if you holidayed at home or a world map if you went abroad (either buy a real map or just print it off Google). Cut the map to fit the photo frame.

Thread the needle and use it to poke a line of holes in the map roughly along the route you took from your house to your holiday destination. Then sew along the route and finish with an x at your destination. Sew cool!

Decorated Drift Wood

This is a great way to make use of any bits of driftwood you find on the beach to turn into a cool display. If you get busy with your imagination and make the colours really bold you'll love the way it brightens up your room.

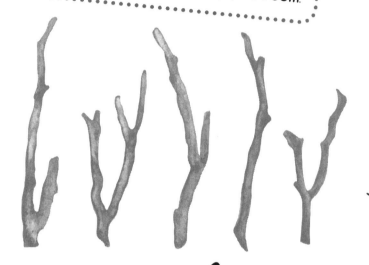

you'll need...

Driftwood Sticks
Brightly coloured paint
Paintbrush
Glass vase

now make it....

Lay the sticks out and take some time painting bright colours on each of them.

Because the sea and sun have bleached the wood you'll fine it has a smooth yet uneven surface that is really nice to work with. Try painting rings around each stick in colourful bold stripes.

Then when they have dried, load them into your glass vase to make a really beautiful and bright natural room decoration.

BFF SUMMER BUCKET LIST

NOW'S the time to get together your must-do bucket list of seasonal fun before the summer ends.

you'll need...

Imagination
A best friend
A ruler
A pencil
A sharpie
A large piece of paper or cardboard
Drawing pins

now make it....

Write the words "BEST FRIENDS SUMMER BUCKET LIST" with a sharpie at the top of your paper/card. Then use a ruler to make some really faint lines on your paper which you'll use as a guide for writing your list

On a separate scrap of paper start scribbling down all your ideas. They can be grand and adventurous or frivolous and fun. Here are a few ideas to get you started :

Pull an all-nighter together
Talk in different accents for a day
Get manicures
Prank call friends
Carve your initials on a tree
People watch at a park
Go on an epic road trip
Take a fashion risk together
Read the same book together
Marathon a tv box set

Once you have finalised your list use your sharpie to write it onto your paper or card. Pin it up on your walls and as the summer unfolds get ticking off that list!

My summer bucket list

Painted Pineapple Party Fun

you'll need...

1 pineapple (1 each for whoever is joining in)
colourful acrylic paints
paint brushes
foam brushes

now make it....

First use the foam brush to coat the palm leaves (that's the tall spiky leaves at the top) in a bright base colour. Don't worry if you can't do every tiny little bit just get some good coverage. Then use a smaller paint brush to do the details and fill in the nooks and crannies. Paint the leaves a single colour or experiment with bold stripes.

It's just the top leaves you are doing, don't try to decorate the actual pineapple itself as the paint won't take well.

you could use some pins to hold a pair of sunglasses or headband onto your painted pineapple to give it a summer look. I can't tell you how cool/funny these look. you can set them up all over the place in unlikely situations and do some really funny snapchats and instagrams ..especially if you give them names/characters. Plus when the fun is finished you can eat them too!

GET READY FOR SUMMER

summer star gazing sleep over

okay this one is super-simple, it's great fun and also a cheeky excuse to persuade your mum and dad to let you have some friends over!

now make it....

When the sun goes down get yourself out into the garden or yard with your friends. Lay out the ground sheet and set up with your blankets and pillows. Lie flat on your back and look out into space. If you're lucky you'll see a shooting star....... if you do, don't forget to make a wish!

Take time to look carefully at the stars and you'll start seeing the patterns they make. These are called constellations and they have special names like The Bear, The Big Dipper & The 7 Sisters.

Look out for the North Star it's one of the brightest stars in the sky. If you want to find out more print off a star map on Google so you can identify what you are seeing. Lie back and take it all in.

you'll need...

A clear night
A couple of friends
A ground sheet/blanket
some warm blankets & pillows

GET READY FOR SUMMER

Good Vibes - Good Morning

This is a really good way to start your day. It's all about 'visualisation' and helps you answer the question "HOW DO I WANT TO FEEL TODAY?"

the first thing...

to do is sit down somewhere quiet in a cross legged position. Get comfortable, close your eyes and slowly take a deep breath. Let your breath out slowly and feel your body begin to relax. Keep on breathing and take the time to notice your breathing. Don't change it, just notice it.

Next try to think of a word or words that describe how you want to feel today. Think positive. Words like 'kind', 'happy', 'peaceful', 'confident' & 'brave' are all good thoughts. What's important is to think about how you want to feel. Breathe in & Breathe Out 10 times say the words out loud and send the feeling you have chosen out into the world.

Open your eyes. Sit for a moment before getting up and enjoying the kind of day you have chosen to live.

Daily Running Routine

With longer days and warmer weather summer is a great time to improve your overall health and fitness.

You don't need to be a super athlete or fitness freak. Just getting outdoors and moving around will increase your overall well-being. Try this running routine but don't stress. If it's too much just settle for a fast walk. Even that will do you good.

first up...

make sure you've got a decent pair of running shoes. Get outside and start off with a warm-up of walking at a comfortable pace for 5 minutes. Move into a slow jog for 3 minutes and, if you feel you can, gradually pick up your pace.

continue your run for another 10 minutes, feeling free to slow down or walk if you need to. Finish with a 3 minute slow jog, or walk to cool down.

while you are jogging try not to swing your arms high and across the body. Avoid doing all your running on hard road surfaces, instead try running on soft park trails to reduce injury risk and feel less fatigued.

Taking photos is fun & free. Grab your camera or your phone and get started with these ideas.

cool Photo Projects

now do it....

Project #1: Self Portraits.
Take one self-portrait at the end of every day for a month that shows your emotions. Think about how you feel and show it on your face. Try not to take the perfect selfie. Be more honest with how your day has been and how you express that feeling. Then just take your pic and move on. Add comments if you can to create a month long visual diary of emotions which you can look back over and, if you like, print out to make a piece of art.

Project #2: A Day In The Life.
Pick a friend or member of your family. Stick with them and shoot their whole day (check they are ok with this first!). At the end of the day choose just 10 pictures that hang together to tell the story of 'A day in the life of.'

Random Acts Of Kindness

If you understand the meaning of the saying 'giving is better than receiving' you'll already know that random acts of kindness can be a lot of fun.

Below is a list of simple low-key ways to make someone, somewhere feel better by a little thing you do. It won't cost you anything but your time ..

 now do it....

★ Give someone a compliment.
★ Hold the door open for someone.
★ Let someone go in front of you in the queue.
★ Stand up for someone who is being bullied.
★ Call your grandparents just to say hi!
★ Go for a walk, take a bag and pick up any litter you see.
★ Leave extra change in the vending machine.
★ Help someone in need with their bags.
★ Send an email to someone to show your appreciation or thanks
★ Use your manners. Say please, thank you and excuse me.
★ Help your younger brother or sister with homework.
★ Help around the house without being asked to do so.

Glow Balloons

you'll need...

Regular party balloons
Glow sticks (the shortest ones you can find)

These luminous balloons are brilliant fun for sleepovers and parties. Take them outside in the garden to play/chill with on a summer's night.

now make it....

First get your glow stick and crack it to activate the light (you don't need to do this for all sticks, just check the instructions).

Gently insert the glow stick into the hole in the neck of the balloon and wiggle/stretch the balloon to get the stick right inside and away from the hole where you blow.

Blow the balloon up. Tie off the end and get some glow in your garden (great in your bedroom too!)

GET READY FOR SUMMER

LUSH IN THE SUN

HAIR & SKIN IDEAS

ENDLESS SUMMER

GET READY FOR SUMMER

Go all out summer with this cool homemade lemonade lip balm.

Lemonade Lip Balm

you'll need...

3 teaspoons beeswax
3 teaspoons coconut oil
1 teaspoon cocoa butter
1 teaspoon shea butter (try The Body Shop)
15 drops of edible lemon essential oil
3 small eye cream jars

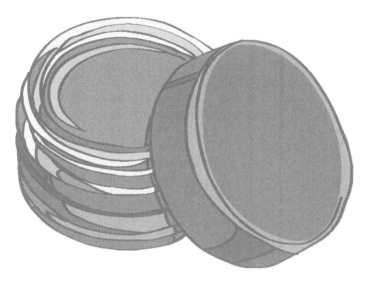

now make it....

Combine the beeswax, coconut oil, cocoa butter and shea butter in a glass bowl. Sit the bowl in a saucepan filled with 5cm of water and gently heat until all the ingredients are melted (you might need an adult to help you with this).

Remove the glass from the saucepan add 15 drops of lemon oil to the mixture and quickly combine before the mixture begins to harden.

Pour the mixture into the jars and allow to cool until the contents have hardened.

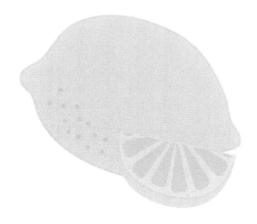

DIY (NO) Beach Hair

Even if you don't make it to the beach this year there's nothing stopping you getting that beach-beautiful tasseled hair look.

you'll need...

500ml hot water
1 teaspoon salt
1 teaspoon coconut oil
1 teaspoon water based hair gel or leave-in conditioner
spray bottle

now make it....

Put all the ingredients into the spray bottle and give it a good shake. spray into damp hair and twist sections of hair as you spray, then let your hair dry naturally.

If you want it to look more extreme spray the mixture onto wet hair and pile it into a bun. when it's nearly dry take out the bun and scrunch your hair in sections.

GET READY FOR SUMMER

Flip Flop Foot Scrub

With the summer coming you need to give your feet a bit of love and get them ready to feel the fresh air in flip flops. and this sugar lemon foot scrub will do nicely.

you'll need...

200g granulated white sugar
20ml almond or coconut oil
2 drops lemon essential oil

now make it....

Combine the sugar, almond/coconut oil & lemon oil together until you have a nice soft scrub. Transfer to a bowl and put to one side while you soak your feet for a few minutes in the bath or a basin of water. This will soften the skin and prepare it for exfoliation.

After your feet have soaked for a bit use your hand to scoop out some of the scrub. Rub it all over your feet using a scrub brush or work it in with your hands.

Place your feet back in the water, let them soak for a bit, then use your hands to help rinse the homemade sugar scrub off. Lift your feet out of the water and dry them off with a towel.

If you want to seal in the moisture then rub some foot cream into your feet afterwards. Your skin will feel slightly oily side until you dry off, after which your feet should feel smoother.

Fake Tan Tips

Everybody loves to have that summer sun-kissed glow and there's no quick (or safer) way to get it than with a little bit of fake tan.

Whichever type of tan you use here are some tips that will help you get that all-over even glow!

★ Before you start make sure your skin isn't dry. Patchy or dry skin doesn't take colour well. Don't try to put too much on at one time. Squeeze a small amount into the palm of your hand (about a 50p coin size)

★ Once you begin make sure you work quickly: starting from your shoulders apply the fake tan to both shoulders and arms using circular and then vertical movements up and down the arms. Avoid the elbows and stop at the wrists.

★ For legs & bums working from your bottom down, again with circular and vertical moves to get even coverage. Miss out the knees and stop just above the ankles.

★ For all the tricky bits like feet, ankles, hands and wrists mix a small amount of moisturiser and tan in your hand at the same time and work the mixture gently onto these bits and the surrounding areas.

★ Feet and ankles are always the worst areas so take special care to blend and don't forget to work it between the toes and fingers too

★ Wait the prescribed amount of time to see results and then rinse off. Make sure you read the instructions on your tanning product carefully and follow those instructions, even if they differ from the top tips mentioned here.

COCONUT & COFFEE BODY SCRUB

Body scrubs are a must if you want to get your skin looking its best for the summer and homemade DIY ones are some of the best of all.

Body scrubs help by giving your skin a nudge to encourage it to shed its old cells and reveal the healthier skin underneath.

you'll need...

200g coarsely ground coffee
300g Epsom salt
180ml coconut oil
1 teaspoon vanilla extract
1 mason jar

now make it....

First combine the coffee and salt together. Add the coconut oil and the vanilla extract. Stir really well and store in your jar. It will keep for at least a few months and is a great DIY gift idea too.

When you are ready to use it do so on damp skin (it's easiest just to stand out of the shower while you scrub all over and then rinse off).

Try using an exfoliating mitt with the scrub (although you'll need to put it in the wash afterwards because of the coffee!). Give yourself a good rinse and dry off.

Do this a few times over the weeks and you'll start to feel the difference in your skin.

Natural Hair Highlights

If you want california-girl sun-kissed hair the natural way, this is a super easy & cheap DIY solution.

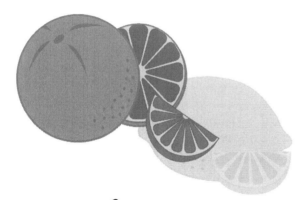

you'll need...

200ml lemon juice
200ml orange juice
50ml warm water
60ml hair conditioner
jug
spray bottle
A sunny day

now make it....

combine the lemon juice, orange juice, warm water & hair conditioner together in a jug then pour into a spray bottle.

spray the mixture over all your hair and give it a few light brushes. Find somewhere to hang-out in the sun for an hour. you'll need to be in direct sunlight so make sure you cover up your skin or use sunscreen.

After this wash your hair with lots of conditioner as the fruit juice can dry your hair out (so you want to put the moisture back in).

you'll need to do this a few times over the summer to see a change but it will work, just give it time.

GET READY FOR SUMMER

Natural Chocolate Bronzer

Forget using chemical laden bronzers which can cause irritation and skin break-outs. Stay natural with this cocoa bronzer that's jam-packed with natural anti-oxidants and smells great too.

you'll need...

Natural unsweetened cocoa powder
A glass bowl
Makeup brush

now make it....

First tip some cocoa powder into the bowl. Then use your makeup brush to gently give yourself an all over bronze glow. Use a little at a time and tap any excess powder off the brush each time you apply. You can use a blusher brush or, if you want more control, use a concealer brush.

Depending on the tone of your skin you can experiment by adding a little ground nutmeg and cinnamon too. Just keep it light and natural and don't worry if you don't get it right straight away just wash it off and start again.

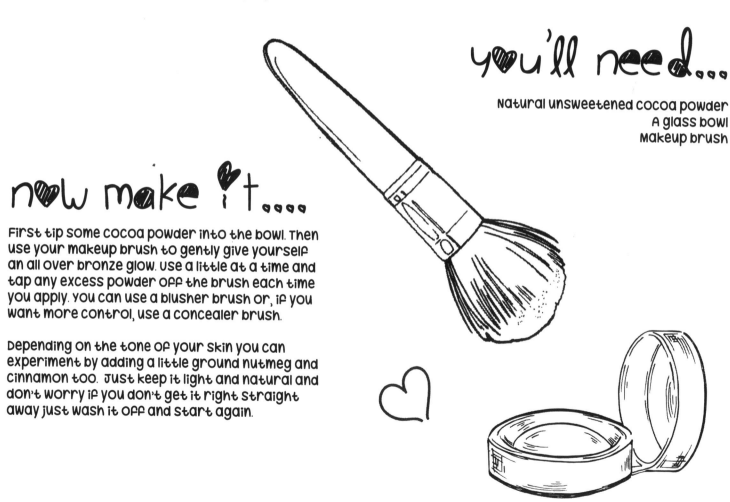

GET READY FOR SUMMER

HOLIDAY D.I.Y. FASION

spiral Tie-Dye vest

For this cool 'beach cover-up' buy yourself a T which is bigger then you usually go for.

you'll need...

A plain white t-shirt
Tie Dye kit
scissors
Rubber bands

now make it....

To get started first of all pinch your shirt wherever you want the center of your swirl to be then twirl your shirt around your pinch until it's compact.

Now comes the tricky bit .divide your shirt into 6 sections using rubber bands. Then, following the dye kits instructions, squirt the dye over each section (making sure you don't overlap your colours). Put your T-shirt in a plastic bag and leave it over night. Give it a good rinse in the bath and then put it in the washing machine on a hot wash.

Hang your T out to dry and then for the final bit take your scissors and cut off the sleeves to make your vest. cut it really low down the sides if you want a loose look.

Polka Dot Daisy Dukes

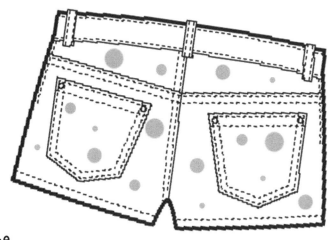

now make it....

Pour some fabric paint into a shallow dish or on to a plate. Lay your shorts out on a clean flat surface then use your ruler as a guide while you dip in the circular foam brush and create lines of tiny polka dots on your jeans. The lines don't need to be perfect (in fact it's better if they're not) the ruler is just there to give you a guide.

Once you have done one side of the shorts, let the paint dry for a few minutes before turning over and doing the other side ..and that's it ..a new look for your shorts. super easy.

You don't have to limit this DIY to dots. You could use a small heart stencil or any other shape you like to customize your jeans.

you'll need...

your favourite denim cut off shorts
white fabric paint
tiny circle foam brush (any craft store will have these)
ruler

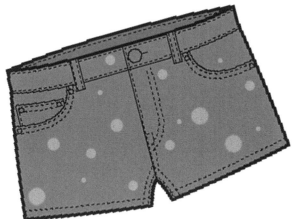

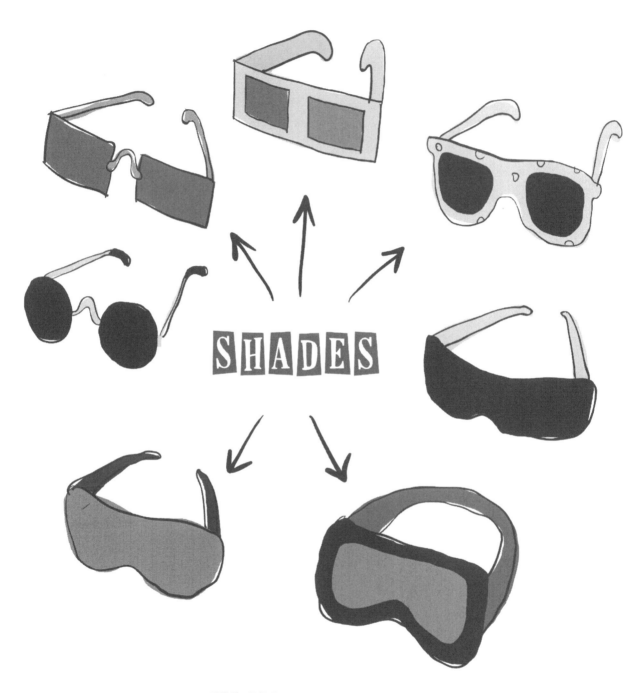

SHADES

customized sunglasses

Here's a cute, quick and easy way to make sure you are rocking a pair of shades that no one else will have this summer.

Dress-up diamantes and jewels are really cheap to buy. You can pick these up in lots of budget stores like Poundland (which is also a good place to get cheap sunglasses too)!

you'll need...

small jewels
cheap sunglasses
hot glue gun

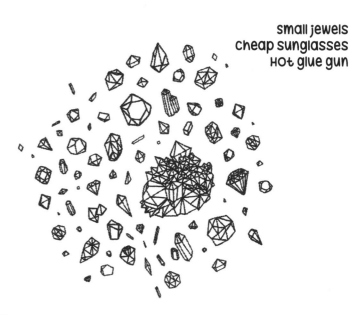

now make it....

Sketch out a few ideas and once you have decided on your design get your glue gun and heat it up. Once it's ready dab glue on the backs of the jewels so that you can stick them on the sunglasses. Arrange the jewels however you like following your design and then stick them down. This is a one-of-a-kind design that will put everyone else in the shade!

Pimp your pumps

you'll need...

A pair of white pumps or sneakers or baseball boots
A selection of coloured sharpies

now make it....

clean up your shoes as much as you can with a damp cloth and let them dry off.
Take your sharpies and make tiny coloured dots all over the pumps. use as many colours as you like to get bright multi-coloured coverage all over.

The finished result will look fresh & summery and will breathe some life into old white pumps which aren't white enough to wear anymore.

Button Bag

This is a cute way to customise a spare canvas bag, purse or pencil case.

you'll need...

A canvas bag, purse or pencil case
A needle & thread
A collection of mixed buttons (you can buy a bag of mixed buttons on ebay for less then a £1)

now make it....

Lay out your buttons and figure out how much coverage you want on the item your have chosen to decorate. You may want to cover the whole thing with buttons, or just a half, or a corner. If you are using a large bag and have enough space you might want to arrange the buttons in the shape of a heart to make it stand out. (If you do decide on a shape it's best to try to draw a really faint outline on the bag first so you can follow the shape).

Then get sewing. There's not magic to this, just thread up your needle and sew the buttons on one by one. Tying each button firmly before cutting the thread and staring on a new one.

bangle wraps

you'll need...

A set of bangles
Multi-coloured embroidery thread
strong glue
Toothpick
scissors

now make it....

Dip the toothpick in a little glue and dab a drop onto a small area of the bangle. Fix the end of the embroidery thread onto the glue and start wrapping it tightly around the bangle. Keep on wrapping tightly and then use your fingers to push the sections together to make sure you get complete coverage. continue wrapping until you get to the end.

To finish off dip the toothpick in the glue again and dab a dot onto the last part of the bangle. wrap the last of the thread tightly on top of the glue and trim off the loose ends.

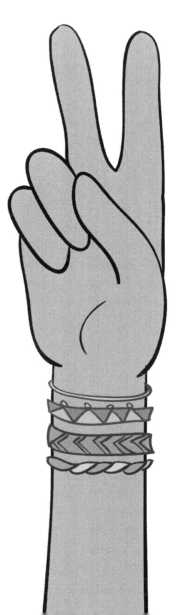